Shark Life

Funny & Weird

Sea Creatures

Funny & Weird Animals Series

By

P. T. Hersom

Shark Life Funny & Weird Sea Creatures

By P. T. Hersom

First Published, 2013

Printed in the United States of America

Hersom House Publishing, 3365 NE 45th St, Suite 101

Ocala, Florida 34479 USA

This book is dedicated to my boy Gabriel, who daily gives me inspiration to share more about the wonderful animals that we share our world with.

Love ya Gabriel

Sharks!

Sharks are fish that have been around a long time, even before dinosaurs existed, over 400 million years ago. Originally called sea dogs by the early 16th century sailors, the name shark first stuck with this fish when in 1569 English naval commander and merchant, Sir John Hawkins displayed a shark in London for people to see.

Most sharks are cold-blooded animals which mean their body temperature changes with the temperature of the environment around them and most live in warmer seawaters throughout the world. However two sharks, the River Shark and the Bull Shark can even survive in freshwater too.

One thing that makes sharks different from other fish is that they do not have bones; instead they have cartilage in their body. Now cartilage is a flexible tissue found in people and animals, like in our ears and noses, or if you like fried chicken, the breast piece and the leg have cartilage in them. Yummy!

There are over 400 kinds of sharks and many different sizes from the small Dwarf Lanternshark which is 7 in/18 cm long, to the huge Whale Shark that grows to 50 ft/15 m in length. All sharks have gill slits on the sides of their heads, ranging from 5 to 7 slits, which are used for breathing. Oxygen is pulled from the water as it passes over the gills and through the mouth.

They lose over 10,000 teeth over their life time on average, because of having no roots like our teeth; they are attached only to the gums and not the jaw bone. Their teeth grow in rows ranging from 5 to 15 rows, so when a tooth is lost a tooth from a behind row moves forward to fill the cap. No visits to the dentist, now that would be nice!

A shark's skin appears to be smooth but is actually rough like sandpaper and made of placoid scales which make its skin tough, and therefore used in making leather products like cowboy boots and purses.

Where Do Baby Sharks Come From?

Well shark babies come from their mother of course! However, different from other bony fish, sharks fertilize their eggs while still inside the mother shark. The daddy shark has claspers that extend from the pelvic fin, which transfer sperm to the mommy shark fertilizing her eggs.

With most sharks, when the baby sharks are born, called pups, they already have a full set of teeth and immediately leave their mother to take care of themselves. However, with a few species of sharks they lay their eggs in the water like other fish. The egg case, which is leather tough, protects the growing baby shark. Once discarded by the shark pup, the egg case is sometimes found washed up the beach and commonly called a mermaid's purse. Weird!

Sharks Are Sensitive Creatures

Did you know sharks have five physical senses just like we do? They can smell, taste, see, hear and feel, plus sense vibrations and electricity! Funny. All these abilities combine to make them fierce predators.

For example, they can smell one drop of blood in 25 gal/100 l of water and up to .25 m/.4 km away! And their taste buds are in their mouths, instead of on their tongues like ours. They see things in color like we do, and their eyes dilate and contract to control the amount of light coming into the eye. They see well in dim light, just like cats do, because of a mirror like layer on the back of the eye. This layer increases the power of incoming light, enhancing their ability to see.

Sharks hear sounds through little pores located on top of their head. They can tell from what direction the sound is coming from and hear low frequencies well. They feel vibrations in the water through their skin, which enables them to detect a possible meal, such as injured fish that are thrashing in the water.

Now for the electricity sense, sharks have the weird ability to sense electromagnetic fields, which is electricity emitted in little amounts by every living creature. They can detect electric fields greater than any other animal, and use it to find prey and navigation.

Sharks Sink!

Swim, swim, swim or sink, sink, sink! Almost all sharks must swim in order to breathe and cannot even take a short nap without sinking! This is because sharks are missing swim bladders. Bony fish have gas filled swim bladders for buoyancy, this is what keeps them floating within the water and not hitting the bottom. Instead, sharks are equipped with an oily oversized liver, usually around 30% of their total body weight, which does provide some buoyancy because the oil in the liver is lighter than water. However, it's not enough on its own, they must keep swimming.

Funny though, two sharks have found a way around it, the Sand Tiger Shark swallows air into its tummy and that forms a make-shift swim bladder, and the Nurse Shark is capable of pumping seawater across their gills which allows them to just rest on the bottom and still breathe.

Weird but true, scientists have discovered that in most sharks, if you turn them over and rub their nose they will go into a tonic immobility state; this is like being paralyzed and unable to move! This generally lasts around 15 minutes before the shark wakes up. Scientists use this technique to further test and study shark behavior.

Basking Shark

Size: Up to 40 ft/12 m in length.

Where they live: Worldwide throughout the arctic and temperate waters.

What they like to eat: Zooplankton such as fish eggs, small crustaceans and larvae.

Tell Me More

Now this is one big mouth! The Basking Shark is one of only three large filter-feeding sharks and is the second largest fish in the world. It's seen swimming with its mouth open a lot, not because it likes to talk all the time, but to cause a constant flow of water. Food is pulled from the water by gill rakers that are attached to the shark's gill slits. These rakers can strain 2000 tons of seawater per hour. That's what I would call a zooplankton buffet.

Blacktip Reef Shark

Size: 6 ft/1.8 m in length.

Where they live: Tropical coral reefs of the Pacific and Indian Oceans.

What they like to eat: Small fish, shrimp and octopi.

Tell Me More

This shark likes to be in shallow water over coral reefs and sandy inshore waters, seeing their blacktip dorsal fin skimming the water's surface is a common sight. No need to be scared though, shy and timid they pose little danger to people unless stirred up by food. Although a saltwater fish, they're known to enter brackish and freshwater areas.

Blue Shark

Size: 12 ft/3.8 m in length and up to 862 lb/392 kg in weight.

Where they live: Worldwide in tropical and temperate waters

What they like to eat: Small fish, squid, cuttlefish and octopi.

Tell Me More

The Blue Shark's slender body makes it a fast swimmer. Its extended tail fin provides swimming power as the tail moves side-to-side. These sharks are among the fastest swimming sharks in the world and can even leap out of the water. Some have been recorded to swim at 43 mph/69 km/h in short bursts.

These sharks migrate great distances each year from the Caribbean Sea, following the east coast of the USA northward, then east across the Atlantic Ocean to Europe, southward to the African coast, and then back to the Caribbean. That's a lot of miles!

The Blue Shark has earned the nickname "Wolves of the Sea" through their working together as a "pack" to herd prey into groups from which they can easily feed. Even though good hunters, they have to watch out for Killer Whales, Sea Lions and other sharks such as, the White Shark and Shortfin Mako that like to eat them.

Bull Shark

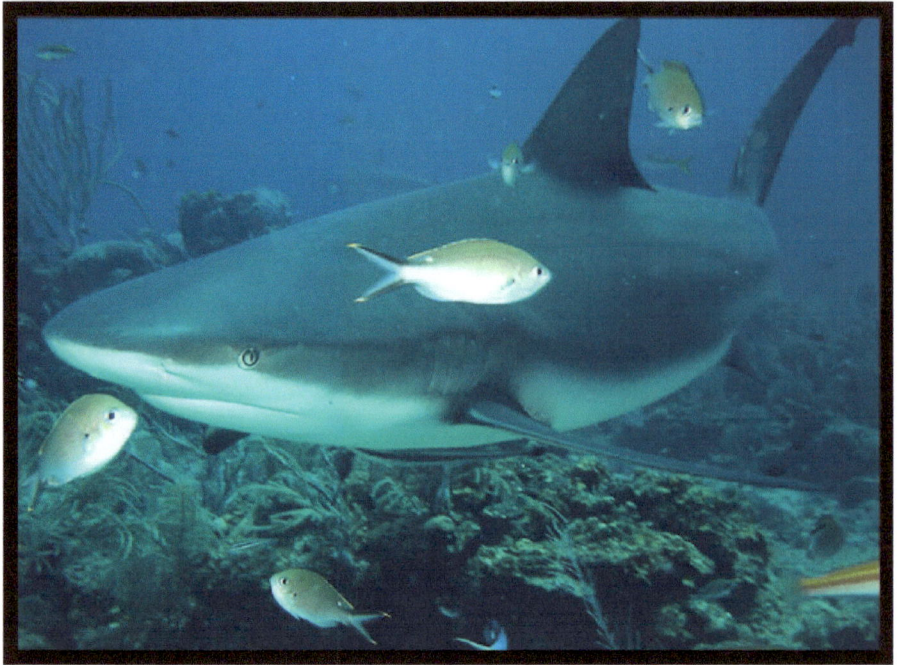

Size: Up to 11.5 ft/3.5 m in length and 500 lb/ 230 kg.

Where they live: Worldwide in shallow coastal waters and rivers, even brackish and freshwater.

What they like to eat: Fish, dolphins, birds, turtles, rays, crustaceans and other sharks.

Tell Me More

A Bull Shark's name comes from their stocky appearance and their aggressive, unpredictable behavior. They live in shallow waters and can swim very fast, plus are extremely territorial. So if an animal enters their territory they aggressively attack it. Bull Sharks are thought to be one of two species of sharks responsible for the Jersey Shore attacks of 1916, which inspired the novel and movie "Jaws", the other species being the Great White Shark.

The Bull Shark can live in both saltwater and freshwater, and can travel far up into rivers and lakes. It has been found as far up as Illinois, which is 1,750 m/2800 km into the Mississippi River in the United States, and 2,500 m/4000 km up the Amazon River in South America, and found in Lake Nicaragua in Central America. These guys can be found almost anywhere and that's no bull!

Carpet Shark

Size: Up to 10 feet in length.

Where they live: Tropical waters of the western Pacific Ocean and eastern Indian Ocean.

What they like to eat: Mollusks, fish and crustaceans.

Tell Me More

The Carpet shark also called the Wobbegong Shark get their name from the strange ornate patterns that cover their skin, giving them the appearance of a carpet. This built in camouflage is further enhanced by little weed like whiskers that surround their mouths and act as sensory barbs. They are a bottom dwelling shark and mainly are seen on the ocean floor resting. They do not pose a threat to humans unless they are provoked.

Cookiecutter Shark

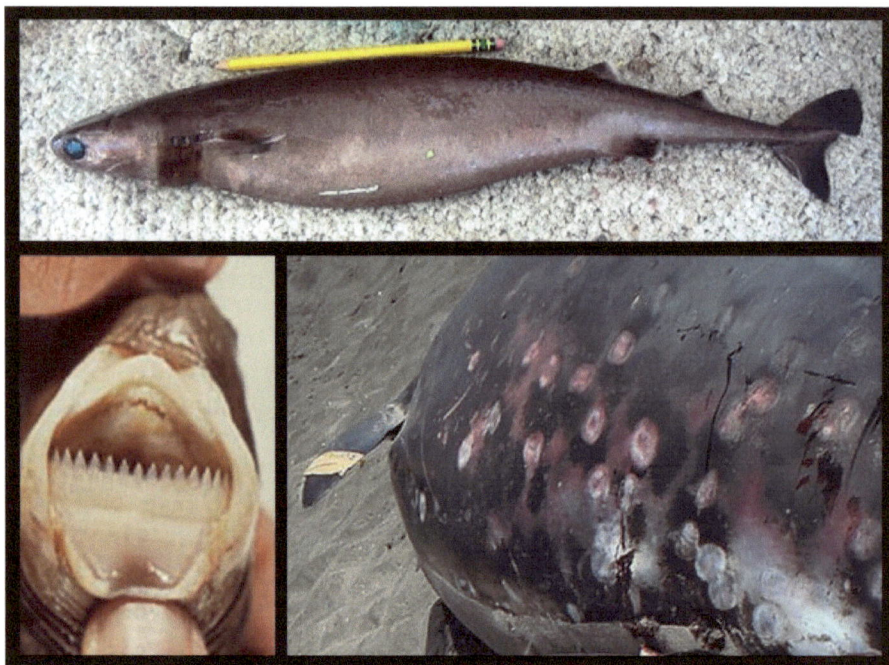

Size: Up to 22 in/56 cm in length.

Where they live: Worldwide in warm oceanic waters.

What they like to eat: Fish, squid, whales, dolphins, stingrays, sharks and seals.

Tell Me More

This shark is also known as the Cigar Shark because of its brown color and light emitting photophores covering its belly, and the dark brown "band"(like a cigar band), around its gill slits. This gives it an unique feeding advantage.

Prey is attracted to the shark from the light given off by the glowing photophores, which make it appear like a small fish. Just when the larger fish thinks it has found its next meal, powie! The Cookiecutter Shark attaches itself to the prey with razor sharp teeth and sucking lips. Once locked on, it spins its body and removes a cookie shaped piece of flesh from the larger fish, leaving behind a cookie cutter shaped round hole in its side.

In the picture above you can see Cookiecutter Shark bite marks on a beached whale. I guess to a fish not all cookies are sweet, funny.

Dwarf Lanternshark

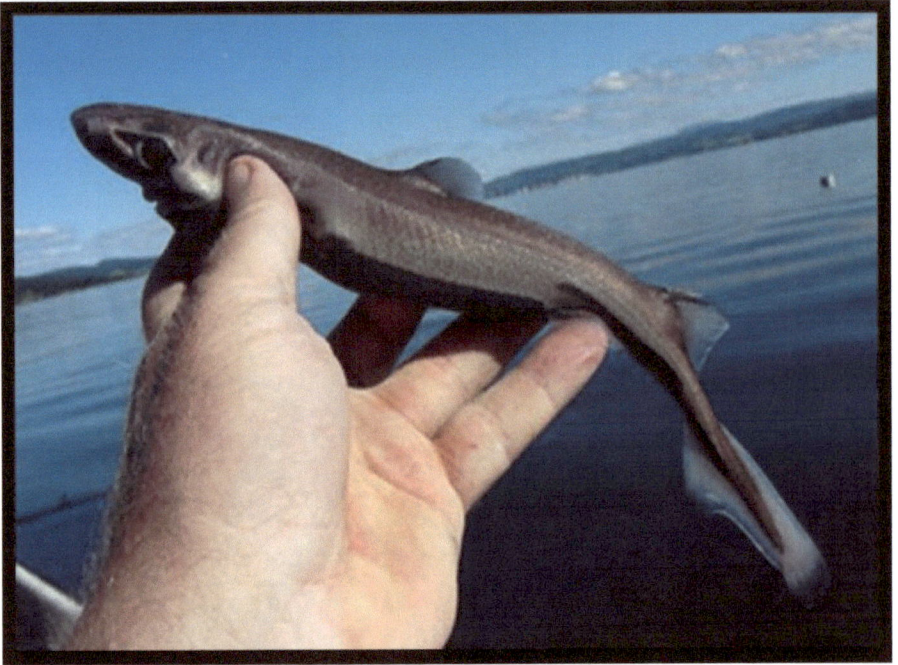

Size: 8.3 in/21 cm in length.

Where they live: In the Caribbean Sea off the coasts of Venezuela and Colombia.

What they like to eat: Small fish, squid and crustaceans.

Tell Me More

The Dwarf Lanternshark is the smallest shark in the world and is found in deeper waters up to 1400 ft/426 m in depth. They get their name from their light producing photophores on their body. These photophores allow them to glow underwater, kind of like a lightning bug or firefly does. Now that's weird.

Great White

Size: Up to 20 ft/6 m in length and weighing 5000 lb/2268 kg.

Where they live: In coastal waters of all oceans of the world.

What they like to eat: Fish and marine mammals such as seals, sea lions and dolphins.

Tell Me More

Along with the Bull Shark they inspired the writing of the novel "Jaws" which later become a blockbuster movie. All for good reason, they are known to be ranked #1 in having the most attacks on humans! From 1990 through 2011 there were 139 Great White Shark attacks worldwide, with 29 people dying.

Great Whites are at the top of the food chain when it comes to sea predators, they are the largest predatory fish. They have up to 3000 teeth that are razor sharp and up to 3 in/7.5 cm long, which they use to tear their prey into bite sized pieces which are swallowed whole.

While hunting the Great White is often seen breaching the water's surface partially or completely out of the water! They can swim up to 25 mph/40 km/h and shoot themselves to more than 10 ft/3 m into the air.

The Killer Whale is their only natural enemy, in 1997 off the coast of California a Killer Whale was seen holding a shark upside down until it went into tonic immobility. The whale held it upside down until the shark suffocated, then it ate the dead sharks liver! Now that's weird!

Goblin Shark

Size: Up to 18 ft/5.4 m in length.

Where they live: In the deep-sea of the Atlantic, Pacific and Indian Oceans.

What they like to eat: Fish, squid, octopus and shrimp.

Tell Me More

The Goblin Shark is one of the weirdest looking sharks alive. Sometimes called a "living fossil' because it descends from a family of sharks 125 million years old. This shark has pink skin, a long flat snout and jaws equipped with nail like teeth.

This shark is rarely seen for it lives at the bottom of the ocean in depths of 4,000 ft/1219 m and is known to be a slow swimmer. So you could probably catch one, if you could find one.

Hammerhead Shark

Size: Up to 20 ft/6.1 m long and weighing 991 lb/ 450 kg.

Where they live: Worldwide in warmer coastal waters and continental shelves.

What they like to eat: Fish, squid, crustaceans, octopus, stingrays and sharks.

Tell Me More

If there was an alien that landed on earth as a fish, the Hammerhead would qualify with its wide thick head and eyes at each end. Hammerheads during the day usually swim together in schools and at night hunt for food by themselves. Their tool shaped head is a deadly weapon used against their prey, for instance, they hit and pin down stingrays with their head to daze them before eating the stingray.

Recreational sport fishermen love to catch Great Hammerheads because they put up such a good fight. Commercial fishermen seek them for their highly valued fins which are used to make shark fin soup, and their liver for making vitamins, their meat ground into fishmeal and the hides used in making leather goods. Nothing like a yummy shark fin!

Nurse Shark

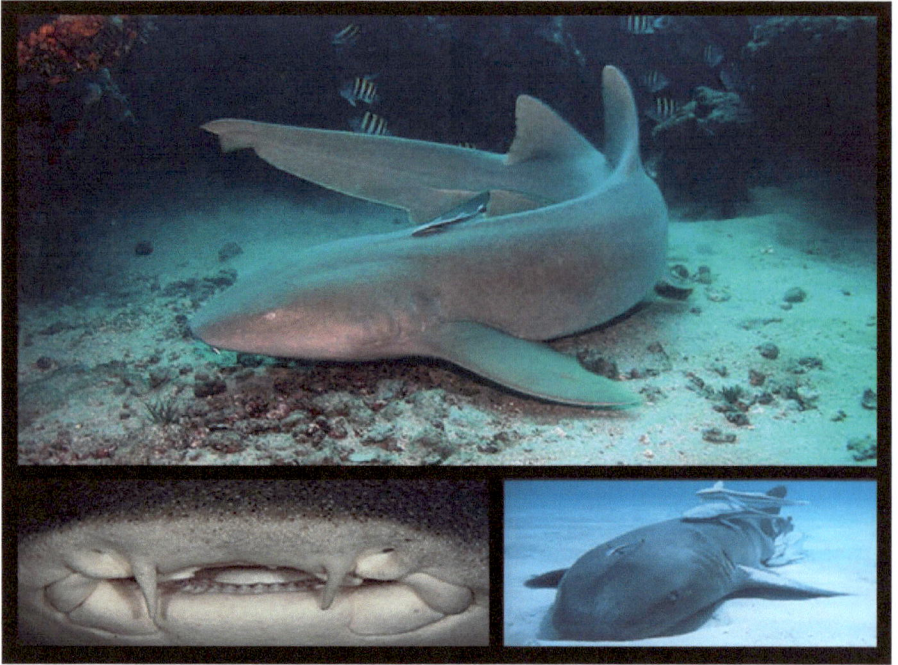

Size: Up to 14 ft/4.3 m and weighing 730 lb/330 kg.

Where they live: Bottom dwelling in tropical coastal waters of the Pacific and Atlantic Oceans.

What they like to eat: Fish, stingrays, octopus, squid and crustaceans.

Tell Me More

The Nurse Shark is nocturnal, which means it is most active at night, and is usually found in groups resting on the sandy bottom, in caves, or among rock crevices in shallow water during daylight hours. They have barbels around their mouth, which are whisker like organs near their nostrils used to sense taste and touch.

These sharks are small mouthed, but have a large throat which allows it to suck in food at high speed. This allows them to prey on small fish that are resting at night, fish too fast for the sluggish nurse shark to grasp during the day. Even hard shelled conches are flipped over, and the snail sucked out with powerful force.

Nurse Sharks are docile and generally harmless to people unless provoked. In which case, they can deliver a powerful clamping bite, causing nasty bruises, and stubbornly refuse to let go of the person bit. Therefore, rescuers must often pull the shark and the person from the water to pry its mouth open to release its victim. So don't try to play doctor with a Nurse Shark.

Shortfin Mako Shark

Size: Weighing up to 1300 lb/590 kg and 13 ft/4 m in length.

Where they live: In temperate tropical waters throughout the oceans of the world.

What they like to eat: Squid, sharks, porpoises, and fish such as tuna, mackerel and swordfish.

Tell Me More

Commonly called the Mako Shark, this shark is the fastest swimmer among sharks, attaining speeds of 46 mph/74 km/h and recorded to travel distances of 1320 miles/2130 km in only 37 days. That's averaging 36 miles/58 km a day! They're a sought after game fish because of their fighting nature and breaching ability, leaping above the water's surface to as much as 20 ft/6 m in the air!

The Shortfin Mako has wicked looking teeth which it uses to tear off chunks of flesh from its prey. They hunt by swimming below their prey and then attacking from underneath at high speed lunging vertically up. Though a fierce hunter this top predator can encounter dangerous prey. Fishermen have found Shortfin Makos with broken off Swordfish bills stuck through their gills and eyes! It appears these sharks sometimes try to bite off more than they can chew.

Spiny Dogfish Shark

Size: Up to 49 in/124 cm in length.

Where they live: In temperate shallow waters offshore worldwide.

What they like to eat: Fish, octopus, shrimp, jellyfish, squid, crabs and sea cucumbers.

Tell Me More

The Spiny Dogfish Shark is the most abundant shark in the seas. They like to swim in schools with other sharks their same size, staying together as they grow. They have big appetites and are known to give commercial fishermen a hard time by chewing through their nets, thus releasing the "Fresh Catch of the Day" for themselves! Funny.

They are commercially fished for their tasty meat (shown in the picture above), which is used in the popular British plate, "Fish and Chips", plus for their oil and making fish meal. As their name implies, they have spines on their dorsal fins which they use to defend themselves from predators. And could create a nasty cut if you tried to grab one, otherwise they are harmless to people.

Thresher Shark

Size: Up to 25 ft/7.6 m long and weigh 1,100 lb/500 kg.

Where they live: Tropical and cold temperate waters worldwide.

What they like to eat: Squid and small schooling fish.

Tell Me More

Thresher Sharks are known for their long tail which can be as long as their body. They use their long tail when hunting, by encircling schools of fish and then slapping their prey with their tails. This stuns the fish which then may be eaten. Sounds like a "bully" the way it slaps fish around.

Threshers are strong swimmers and can breach the water fully and even make turns in mid-air like dolphins. They are shy and not considered dangerous to humans, but if you see one don't let him slap you around.

Tiger Shark

Size: Up to 18 ft/5.5 m and weigh 3360 lb/1524 kg.

Where they live: In tropical and subtropical waters around the world.

What they like to eat: Sea turtles, sharks, rays, fish, dolphins, squid, crustaceans and sea birds.

Tell Me More

Named after the tiger like dark stripes down their back, these guys are big and will eat almost anything in their path. Their sharp jagged teeth combined with a saw like action from shaking their head back and forth, easily tear chunks of meat from larger sea animals. Funny but true, often times sport fishermen will find man made items in their stomachs. One shark's stomach revealed two plastic bottles, a baseball, a license plate and a tire!

Whale Shark

Size: Up to 50 ft/15 m in length and weigh over 66,000 lb/30 metric tons.

Where they live: In all warm temperate and tropical waters of the world.

What they like to eat: Plankton, krill, squid, fish larvae and small fish.

Tell Me More

This is one big fish, in fact, the largest shark in the world. Can you find the diver next to the Whale Shark in the upper picture? Good thing for him these sharks like to eat plankton and not meat. The shark's mouth is wide open because it is sucking in plankton from the sea water, which are tiny microscopic animals and plants.

As the diver found out Whale Sharks are gentle giants and harmless to people.

Zebra Shark

Size: Up to 8 ft/2.5 m in length.

Where they live: In the Western Pacific Ocean around Australia, East Asia and Indonesia.

What they like to eat: Small fish, crabs, shrimp and mollusks.

Tell Me More

The Zebra Shark is a bottom dwelling shark found among coral reefs and sandy bottoms. It feeds at night and spends most of the day resting on the sea floor. The young sharks have spots and vertical strips from which it gets its name Zebra Shark, as they grow older the strips disappear leaving only the spots. Weird, maybe they should be called Leopard Sharks since they can change their strips, but not their spots? Slow moving and docile the Zebra Shark is not a threat to people.

What Did You Learn Today? Questions

1. The Basking Shark has a big mouth which it uses to eat big fish, true or false?
2. I have black coloring on my dorsal fin and tail. What is my name?
3. The Blue Shark is nicknamed the "Wolf of the Sea" because it growls, true or false?
4. Does the Bull Shark have horns on its head?
5. I'm the "rug looking" Wobbegong Shark, what is my more common name?
6. I like to make cookies from other fish. What is my name?
7. What is the smallest shark in the world? (Hint: Snow White had seven.)
8. True or false, the Great Black Shark has the most recorded attacks on humans?
9. This shark reminds many of Halloween?
10. This shark uses its head like a tool from your toolbox?
11. The Nurse Shark helps hurt small fish, true or false?
12. This shark is the fastest and can jump 20 ft/6 m into the air. What is its name?
13. I like to eat the Fresh Catch of the Day from fishermen's nets. Who am I?
14. You may think I'm a bully because I like to slap other fish. What is my name?

15. A license plate, baseball and a tire where found in a Tiger Shark's stomach, true or false?

16. The Whale Shark is actually a whale, true or false?

17. When it's young the Zebra Shark has stripes on its body, true or false?

What Did You Learn Today? Answers

1) False, it uses it to eat Zooplankton, not big fish.

2) The Blacktip Reef Shark.

3) False, it is because of the sharks working together as a pack to herd prey.

4) No.

5) The Carpet Shark.

6) The Cookiecutter Shark.

7) The Dwarf Lanternshark.

8) False, the Great White Shark has the most attacks.

9) The Goblin Shark!

10) The Hammerhead Shark.

11) False, it eats them.

12) The Shortfin Mako Shark.

13) The Spiny Dogfish Shark.

14) The Thresher Shark.

15) True.

16) False, whales are mammals; the Whale Shark is a fish.

17) True.

Other Books to Enjoy by P. T. Hersom

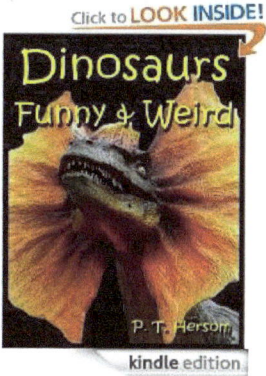

Click to LOOK INSIDE!

Dinosaurs Funny & Weird

P. T. Hersom

kindle edition

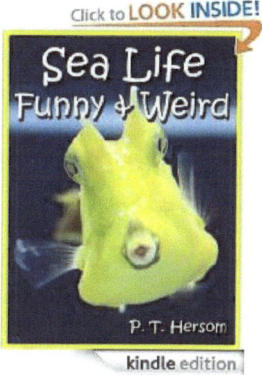

Click to LOOK INSIDE!

Sea Life Funny & Weird

P. T. Hersom

kindle edition

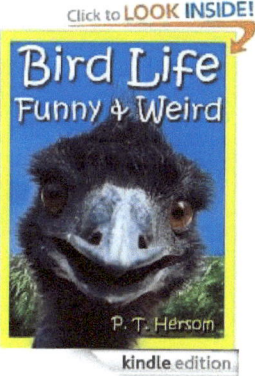

Click to LOOK INSIDE!

Bird Life Funny & Weird

P. T. Hersom

kindle edition

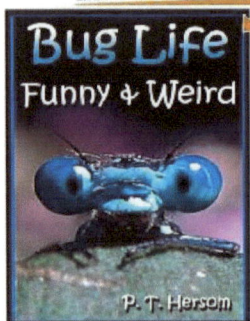

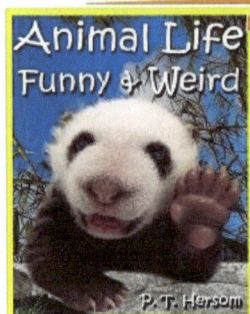

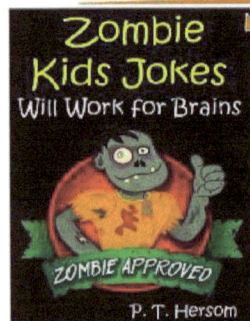

Bug Life
Funny & Weird

P. T. Hersom

kindle edition

Animal Life
Funny & Weird

P. T. Hersom

kindle edition

Zombie
Kids Jokes
Will Work for Brains

ZOMBIE APPROVED

P. T. Hersom

kindle edition

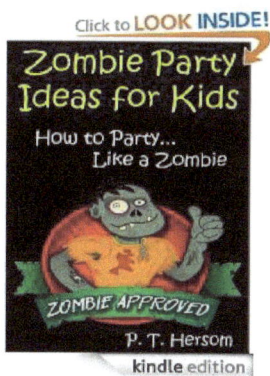

Click to LOOK INSIDE!

Zombie Party Ideas for Kids

How to Party...
Like a Zombie

ZOMBIE APPROVED

P. T. Hersom

kindle edition

Enjoyed the Book?

Thank you for buying this book. I hope that you and your children enjoy reading the book and learning about the animals in the book as much as I did writing it. If you found the book enjoyable, please help me out by posting a review on the Amazon page. Thank you for taking the time to do so. It is very much appreciated.

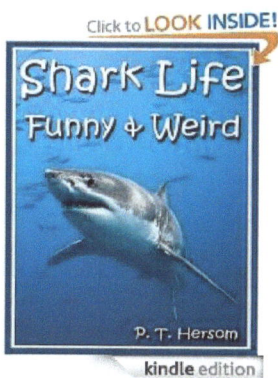

Click to LOOK INSIDE!

Shark Life
Funny & Weird

P. T. Hersom

kindle edition

www.ingramcontent.com/pod-product-compliance
Lightning Source LLC
Chambersburg PA
CBHW041359090426
42741CB00001B/22